for Dan —

MY
NEW
JOB

CATHERINE WAGNER

[signature]

Sonoma State
11/12/09

MY
NEW
JOB

CATHERINE WAGNER

ALBANY, NEW YORK

Cover design by   Rebecca Wolff
Book layout by   Colie Collen

Published in the United States by   Fence Books
                                         Science Library 320
                                         University at Albany
                                         1400 Washington Avenue
                                         Albany, NY 12222
                                         www.fenceportal.org

Fence Books are distributed by   University Press of New England
                                         www.upne.com

and printed in Canada by   Westcan Printing Group
                                         www.westcanpg.com

Library of Congress Cataloguing in Publication Data
        Wagner, Catherine [1969-]
        My New Job/ Catherine Wagner

Library of Congress Control Number: 2009932512

ISBN 13: 978-1-934200-31-5
ISBN 1-934200-31-X

FIRST EDITION

FENCE BOOKS are published in partnership with the University at Albany and the
New York State Writers Institute, and with help from the New York State Council on the
Arts and the National Endowment for the Arts.

CONTENTS

EXERCISES

HOLE IN THE GROUND

EVERYONE IN THE ROOM IS A
REPRESENTATIVE OF THE WORLD AT LARGE

ROARING SPRING

MY NEW JOB

EXERCISES

EXERCISE 3 (11/20/00 PM)

Try not to say it so joltingly. Panorama
and pattern and glorious intention and derailed
streak of yellow up the left eyelid and a cramp in the groin
Who is still awake after I've taken my watch off
Two fingers upward and a thumb clasping
My rabbit my pine trees by a lake and the roots protrude
Here the sexual exercise the embarrassing
Want this bathwater? Yes.
Drum immemorially my heart in my face and hands
Push to the night a tender sacrum
You're taking awhile to drink that beer.
Yeah.
The unlock on the desk & graceful woodhoney chair unsat
Pink, pink pink beep he is calling and strolling the room in rich creaks
A long number quoted and a check will be sent

EXERCISE 5 (11/29/00 PM)

The palegreen frame around the door is very regal when I am drunk
Little animal fetchings
It is different every time & now I see the shadows of my rubber cord
converging shaking doubling as I pull.
I skipped a set.
In this one nought's come up to say. A soreness.
Attending hard a metallic feeling in the nostrils a formality
Still the scary leaf against the window. No movement
in the leaves; all dead, like diorama
Confused circle where the light was on my shut lid.
I completely forgot to put the heater on.
We can fill the hot water bottle. Put the kettle on.
Front room heater snaps and grudges relaxing: turned off

How are you booge? Are you the booge?
I'm the booge.

That's the rule: I have to write down whatever's happened.
Oh is it? I'm going to have a piss on your chest then.

EXERCISE 8 (12/4/00 AM)

Raise up your back like an insect on the face of the nation
He took Miss Mousie on his knee, O say
little mouse will you marry me?
Getting hair cut this morning illegally
I can't afford it
Fourteen fifteen I depend on you and roiling unlap this morn
The mind refrigerated all night
Now to clarify the broth skim off the oil & swallow it is your oil
I must have it shorter so it grows longer in unison
A glory and stern grandeur, which men silently gazed on with wonder
and tears

EXERCISE 1 (11/28/00 PM)

I make the ground ripple and my head red sing
What would be in my chest to hurt me? A leaf crumpled to the window
I lean forward on a nerve ebullient
my sweet alive and roasting in a current
sciatica verboten clockwork nerve
precinctual. Slip off.
Fling off the comfort rims jangle the pane
Hand behind the head the nerve blanks in the shoulder
gray wrangling split shock
a Yucatan of back laid blankenbare
the pudding inside lanced with yards of net
which MY WISH slowly I draw through   the muscle runs out in squares
little cities cube and grow and fluster off in wet drags
& the nerve is broke, disinteger,
cannot call.
Let me know how muscular you are & monster reich & fringed.
Swoopy and familiar
without your limp or slowy back. Asleep.

EXERCISE 7 (12/3/00 PM)

Impression of a deluxe life
Pur, pum the heater double folded white coverlet warm room
Good for M the comfortable-with-people to be away
from me. tauten the cord to make it all more urgent

Skipped one and forgot what I thought of
whatever it was wasn't poetry or was better than I could write
"Super reading" I said and I meant it though
I'd never buy the book & I don't know
why he's writing the stories. I stayed awake
the whole time, is why. If they invited us to dinner at their house M
shouldn't have paid for half. Is it all about money? It is when we might
bounce our rent check and M is out drinking—I hadn't told him—It is
natural to feel riled up when I'm breathing hard but I only just calmed
myself so stop it.

EXERCISE 15 (4/8/01 AM)

Put your hand in the womb and let it sprout

Not ready at all just trees between the shutters

EXERCISE 19 (9/1/01 AM)

G oodmorning Sept 1 or 2 2001
   There was a place in the mouth, a sore bit.
   There was a place in the mouth, a bitter place called Carla.
Eating the cartilage off a drumstick

that is kneecap

Let us stop pushing up and up

Let us start pulling up

Pulling pulling push

Am a genius.

Look at those legs.

EXERCISE 6 (12/1/00 AM)

Ah good the left shoulder hurts again
because right shoulder was, and is the wrong one

EXERCISE 21 (11/8/01 AM)
[BACK SEAT OF MINIVAN]

The wheatrows flattened
gold, another dark
combed curve opened
 like a stretchy
machine.
Roseates from the sacroiliac. Thigh hotting up.
A blaze streaks over grass [deforms] stretches in the window
Murmur from the front.
Again the white blaze. I shut to roseblood and blue dots.

EXERCISE 28 (12/17/01 PM)

I politely rise to meet
my knee
As I get sorer in the belly
I hate the knee
am however diligent and strict

EXERCISE 31 (12/29/01 PM)

Would rather be watching TV
      Huge apt and my body in it, one percent
      of it, moving. Monstrous.

Lifting the hips toward the ceiling the air
 below revamps

Yellow reflection
    swells and dives over a hill of glasscurve
    I move my head, yellow pinlight
      grows a hole in its center & sucks together

9 venomous birds V's of beaks
     around the ceiling lamp
 upholding it in round of brass.
Strong and free of attitude
a bracelet around a punch.

What do you think you are going to find out?
I will find out.
Facing the room, I could walk in there
the girl thrown from the lamp

EXERCISE 25 (11/29/01 PM)

I see myself in the television and in the window
   rise up with my glasses
      on and my hair all round me and my
     stripy shirt like water dripping off me
I do 'em so they get easier so at the end I'm just lying here
Quoting myself

M: I didn't get to see you all today.
    I saw you yesterday, but you weren't very good.

EXERCISE 32 (12/30/01 PM)

Just in every rathole, just trying to learn everything at once
I was learning everything at once

EXERCISE 34 (1/3/02 PM)

Snow
starred when I looked straight up
sky dark gray, geese rose
in alarmed soft shh and hasping
long-necked geese
a-gossip all upset

Home I immed. dial
does anyone love me, and Karen does.
Muscle under collarbone hurt today
from fooling with computer.
Look left and up pulls like a bitch
Haven't cleaned the house since Martin left, and living out of the freezer,
   the old food,
and no fresh, and living high alone and secret way up high a cloud ranch
twisted threw me on the bank spurred my own cheek
Cloud at the level of my eye
I was high up in my head with cheek-hollows like the Red Sea
To reward me my email is up
Chelsey, Rebecca with news of a plug from Powell's, and Janet; not bad
   yellowredpearl and interrupting twigs
                  Somebody liked my booooook
      Do I want something scary

an extreme change, so it's obvious what to do

  (dig my way out the rubble, toward the cries)

and make my now golden?

                            fadeproof/waterproof

   I knew I was a sign to myself

       I couldn't see myself except in the mirror

which 1) wasn't me 2) was me backwards was 3) flat was 4) making me

vain or 5) making me embarrassed to go out, that was all a sign to me

   not a sign of me

all along I was alone to that

though everyone saw me

   checking myself out by talking to them

when they checked themselves out in me

I tried to say Oh here have it all

       warm woolen flood   welcomer

        some spider-netting held it back,

  kept growing over my warm and my intention to befriend

       I could use it to disinfect

a wound and it abstracted me, which was salvation.

EXERCISE 41 (1/15/02 PM)

Wanted to be a phenom.
Rolled over & was a phenom on the other side

Sizzled behind my shoulderblade
                dry & sizzled blue
    like a light on in there
    the nerves treed into my skull
    lit up & whamming

Where are you, muscle relaxer.
Vague dirtying round the edges & a thoughtfulness

The ratio of pain to me 11:45 p.m.
is that of celebrity to USA-world
the spotlights & the gossip
anchored in her.

EXERCISE 4 (11/30/00 AM)

Yawn makes the foggy shuddering around my jaws and temples
A bright patch on the wall. What was the point of not connecting?
This is translation: *Hand on the belly* or
                            hand on belly or
                            I feel the pulse in my belly

                Or then there is *stomach*
In 8 hours asleep I drank a small bottle of water. When did I
Between sets or between breaks is the writing
Cannot see my face which feels
                                        widemantled
M singing: "It's the stinkiest poo in the world/
It's a poo/In the world"
Durable renewable and on the floor I
can't remember why to get up—soft round
cars and loamy fog in shuteye

EXERCISE 13 (12/7/00 AM)

Merry Xmas Sarah from Cathy. And to Martin. And to Jon
Heater rattles & pompoms on the backs of my eyes
from looking at the lightbulb
                        Pow! plow! fading purple pomme
Glasses pushed askew by the pillow
One two three four five six seven eight nine 10 there was nothing else
This writing is not a lazy or easy activity Wags
Either build it by main force or shut up and listen for the Old Ones
Go into the kitchen sift together Flour Cardamom Cloves Cinnamon
    and leavening
Wash face insert eyes smear pale goo on pimples
Remember to brush teeth

EXERCISE 33 (1/3/02 AM)

Why don't you work? Is it because you are lazy or do you
think you can't?
The room filled with an even quantity of light.
Sound of a woman talking on television downstairs
Reviewing a friend's friend's book I began a casuistry: should I be positive
and lie, or simply
describe the book, sly damning?   Explain my disapproval?
They're not in bed yet. Derek shut a drawer upstairs. Someone drove by
I might know 'em but I shut the shutters
A hall in white, a floor in blue, a carpet
The joints collaborate & I walk there
I put the heat back on & it is branging
I don't have to listen to these shitballs coming out of your mouth
Nobody has to listen to mine

EXERCISE 38 (1/7/02 PM)

Monster planet buzzing around
the bursting-forth gold flash arrival
Martin Corless-Smith
I will have to cover my eyes
Shy Martin Corless-Smith
Seventy angels with ruthless eyes
maxxing the jets of the plane
massaging the red lights green
as he sways in the back of the cab
I subducted the clouds
from the path of the plane
& they roil & burl up in Kansas
King of the silent Tetons
in white phosphorescence below
enjoy your journey Sir

EXERCISE 26 (12/01/01 PM)

Nothing at all in my head? In my head?
My skinny head up and down in the window
one set of lines vanishes as I
rise, the other as I lower myself

Just because you write these every day doesn't mean the lines can be throwaway

Yes it does

The master spoke, and I caved.
The anti-authoritarian was bossy, and I swayed;
"I try to do what everyone says."
The rightest thing: there wasn't one.
Agreed.

I was caught out two-faced. Yet my
first mask was politeness. That OK?
You're not blonde, are you? glimpse in mirror.
The gussets round my legs don't leak.

Hip too bony to lie on.
Some part about goin' round, inside the shoulder
"Ol' Shouldy" yellow glimmer-line, sequin-line
grimacing around in there
long telephone-wire flails

Button up your vanity.
There's a pocket in your heart for it
shove it in there, and button it bursting down.
What's my ambition? shoulder everybody.
Ol' Shouldy's gusset leaked.
Fakin' it, bum *poom*.

Can't just say "rain" because it's raining.
It's not "rain." Feb 16 heard rain
on car wheels.

EXERCISE 42 (1/21/02 PM)

Breathed & ovulated, breathed & blood fanned out
    Tough new cord so I get stronger
    & the joint will stay in place like a pearl in vaseline
You will always have your heart to listen to rock you
Carrion chewing at myself
Pull down the shoulder   pull down the knee
Harness that yellow thing from my glance
  darted across, & 2–3 purple ball-blotches
I never see anything without the glance before
    printed over it
 my heart vibrates the ceiling
The apt not mine & the carpet's not my fault
I love that.

HOLE IN THE GROUND

Like a mole in the ground I would root that mountain down
I wish I was a mole in the ground

(folksong)

THE ARGUMENT

This book is called Hypneratomachia Fuckphila.
Fuckfila on her journey her new spelling
reminiscent of Chick-Fil-A. Fill the
chick and filler well of ding ding dong.
Fuckin' A. Behold a useful and
profitable book. If you think otherwise,
do not lay the blame on the book, but on
yourself. If you sourly refuse
the new erotic guest, do not despise
the well-ordered sequence nor the fine
well-ordered style. Then in this volume
she falls in love. It is a worthy book, and full
of many ornaments: he who will not read it
is dull of mind. Various things are treated in it
which it would tire me to relate, but accept
the work which offers a cornucopia
emending it should it be incorrect. The End.

WELL IN YOUR CHASM OF FAITH OPPORTUNITY TREE WHY DON'T YOU CRAMPON UP

for Kelly Morse

Down by the BAY
where the muskmelons GROW   back
to my HOME   I dare not
GO   For if I do   My mama
might say

DID YOU EVER SEE AN OSTRICH
    STAPLING WITH A BOSTITCH

DOWN BY THE BAY
can you see
            my home
    where my mama say

Roam   and if I do   My mama

might say

Some
    W H E R E
a place for us
A little stapled us

OH

In the little painting of love
Is a man repairing a fence.

A little crap love-object
And a too-big church in the background
Near the sea
By a strip of valley
Lit up like surgical tape.

Metaphors can incline one
Toward healing thoughts.
I will have your experience.

The ocean uptaken in the wind
Rolls inland.

Heal, heal, fungus on toe,
Heal, toe.

If I lose this job
[I have other skills?/There are other workers].

If we all lose our jobs
We go to Ocean City
And photograph ourselves
As human pyramids.

My grandfather spent the thirties
Thus on the beach.

Abundant poverty to live in. Many years.

Between you and me is chestbone.
No meshing.
So eat my face for hours.

If a poem is active
Its action aborts in you
As colored light flies into black.

Keeps flying
The light from long ago
Until the night-blockade.

So shut the book.

The man who mends the fence
Imaginary

Leaves a space for the caissons to roll
Down valley from sea.

Let me eat your face, neighbor
Who owns the Bagel and Deli on High
And has two children,
Lily and Garrison.

DE PROFUNDIS CLAMAVI, OR DID I SEEK

The fucking isn't interesting

The fucking is friction

The friction is two surfaces
 in contact and moving.

The depths I clam from

out of the depths I cling to you
oh Penis.

Wispy, nispy, nispy, nis

I charge my galley with forget fullness

A galley is a rowed ship

rowed by slaves.

To fuck a disgusting body

  whether it were the person's will or not, and
against my will

Like a hole in the ground I would root that mountain down.

  Root it down so far
  the hole's dismantled

Or continue to allow the whole hole

 to be filled

With an instability (the wavering
                         penis)

Wavery, sweet and blind.

Oh come on up.

Welcome, welcome my one true love.

Welcome, welcome said she.

I trawled my love through a half a dozen maids

and I laid him at the bottom of the sea.

Fallacious = fellatio + delicious

but is delicious
cut grass and oysters

Beachy Head,   if unpleasant

against the rear throat,

the gag reflex you learn to control
in high school

Terrify all comers.

DIVISION OF FIRE

The frictive surface is not the limit of the touching.

Beneath the surface   the private cell   has an

inverse aspect that joins it to
the other cells the lover's
passersby's

Your cock between my asscheeks, the pipe
not yet rolled into the culvert

Culvert protects the road
water runs under the road.

Thus people walk and shake hands
on top of the fucking.

A body dies and can't

any more spread lightning
from the friction surface

into the

connected halls.

The bar magnet [cock] moves

the copper coil irritates into flowthrough

Some of my electrons, they jumped across
Your field braced and fell and quivered

the October cells
hornet inside out.

FOR THE BOYS

Can you imagine dear men
what it is to be a woman being fucked.
The men installing a new gate
—ran past them prickling, face
prickling, back of neck
  sensitive and tight, and they *do*
say something to/about me

                    Now there was
in a transparent skybox
  someone watching my body and giving it
  a score.   I berated myself for letting it
hover; then the man in the orange construction helmet
  crashed through the skybox glass
with his head,
and the transparent box
filled with color and a stone support
under it. I did not make it up.

Will you just fuck me or
will I just fuck without the skybox.
There is no fucking without the skybox.

This part is for girls, college highschool girls

The guy fucks you five eight minutes
you think you are supposed to come
you do not. What's wrong with you?
frigidaire girl.
 "—But prior girl came all the time!"
To have to learn to be pleasing
throws his image
 as successful lover

—image he needs, to continue sexing—

    in doubt.

The problem lies
with you.

This situation   lie on both sides

is the rule. There are exceptions.

Now let us have ceremonial
sex.

Who is the pauper?

I will be.   I will be.

THE YOUNG ASSISTANT TO THE DIRECTOR OF

Sacred Music at the Yale
Divinity School, his name is
Jim, he plays country music
on his guitar, he shops for
guitars but does not buy them,
it is a pleasure to see the fine
guitars and marvel at the
pricetags, the assistant to the director
of Sacred Music has large
eyes, green or blue,
when people are shopping
for guitars and you are on the
escalator at MOMA, in
New York, assessing your
claustrophobia and why the art
in the building is drained of
root or intention
you have a job and a child, are on
vacation from the job, the
child's with his dad, you are
in a museum inhabiting
a body that used to go to museums
and rattle with awe, it is uncomfortable
that the rattle is still, and Jim calls you,
you met on the train
from New Haven, he's a little short,
you like tall men, you're
not alone,

light colors, black-rimmed,
attract your notice, there's mascara
for that, or dark long lashes
and Italian-boy brows.

HELMETEROGENOME

Am in the   "office"   "confession booth"
fantasy place of Transgression

necessary, where am all outside
viewing the woman/my
    "beautiful body," I change her
 clothes many times

and the male is helplessly seduced
    or he seduces

in a sexy wrong place

*

A homeless man sleeps on the church steps in sun
pennies all over him, some tilted to blazing.

That's what he costs.

He's flaccid. I can get him off
the church steps, one phone call—

hot! The balance of power
must be unequal
for the sex to happen fast enough
in fantasy; power permits

someone to move.
Also, inequality
makes the move socially unacceptable sexy
old yuck tent.

*

I'm angry with him, here's how
he approaches: swallows a mouthful
of dirt bitten off the
ground—when he
shits it's the same color as the dirt
not even a baby in it.
The shit pushes him forward.

*

Part of the poem includes:
fucking the penis from
behind it, the point of view of the "man"
his body fucks it, it's split off from him
around it the woman

reshapes him on the inside as breath harnesses blood cells
she fucks his penis.

What a heterosexist poem!

[handwritten annotation: poem comments on itself]

ARTICULATE HOW

I won't say anything
        I can't say
    like this
I WON'T SAY ANYTHING I CAN'T SAY LIKE THIS

To believe in a formula   of angry bangry
when not hungry

say "I've figured out what interrupts" the
        matrix, and the capitalist me
Uncouth! uncouth and tyrannical

In a tyranny of doubt I owe my students
and my suitors.

But all of the suitors
are already mine
all of the time, I have already slept
with all of them. Here's what it was like
sleeping with you—

I dare you to give me pleasure.
THAT IS NOT HOW THAT IS NOT HOW
I'll show you. No I'll finish you.
Go to sleep. I will finish me too.

Who's alive who slept with Ginsberg I could sleep with? so I could sleep
with Whitman. Cassady slept with someone who slept with Whitman

whose germ mobilized my tree.

What you askew I shall askew.
You could offer me lots of split vaginas
and say Hey fee-fee telephone tree
and other gaudy nonsense
because I would not sleep with any of you.
I held myself awoof.

THIS IS A FUCKING POEM

don't expect too much.

Well I expect you to go into the
fucking human tunnel
I'm going.

pink grimy glossed
entabulature, welted
and tattooed. Enfolded in
ropy ceiling-hangings
but it isn't a room,

and bumblingly sliding
out, little legs of

a little girl, bum on the wall/opening

pink legs sticking out like a
hermit crab's, she's coming!

shudder out the little-girl
legs with a little
girl head mostly eyes, no ears,
bug brain, aimless

Send her to school

*Young
girl
Exploring
sexuality*

It's cold, and where should she
go, she will eat her
legs with her mandibles

her eyes will retract inside.

Stroke her riding hood
Settle down, little

nobody will hurtcha

by breaking off your little legs,
six little legs,
if you come.

COMING AND I DID NOT RUN AWAY

STILL not finished review
but productive day and feeling
        GÜT
like a fine mama
        SHÜT
putting down some
        RÜTS
like the lost queen
        TOOT
        TOOT
            TÜT TÜT TÜT
Brand spankin hanky pankin
  new periodical
    in my uterus
                yest I cried
                thought I was going
                NÜTSO
Not So   Ah so?   yes it was just

a periodical
making me illogical
not wrong though
I was not wrong

I saw the "usual turn of phrase"
coming and I did not run away
I lay around

X

I wish I wanted to sleep with you

Your equation is simple

I can form an x shape

Ready to embrace you with arms and legs

Oh, the radio half-life of my

Space in your equation

Sings a song
You half-hear

Any part of me that accepts your cock

Is an expart

Arctic radio

That freeze-dries you
With its song.

A nest of yellowjackets
On the west wall of my rental

They don't die
When they sting you

Bottom-barbed, fuzzy-headed
Angry from way back.

You are very large, full of air
And tied to the top of a building
Plenty of people will
Blow hot air up your pantsleg.

My other half-life
Is not ex-anything.
A radio half-life
You could barely understand
Profoundly and forever
Unslept with
By you $_x$

The equation's parts
Reduplicate around the x

Oh, no one's nice that doesn't want
          something from you
Oh, hand him a photocopy
          of what he wants

I'm lit from below by the copier light
     No one looks good
  lit from below

But I need to make a copy of
     My sat-upon for you
To fold and airplane.

PRO FORMA

for DK

The techniques that are being used are called Natural Fracture Pruning and Coronet Cutting. We are attempting to mimic the jagged edges found on broken branches following storm damage.

[sign Hampstead Heath]

But it's not really a date

But that one, I'll have that one
 too if I want (that guy)

they are all of them
  needling my love.

You womp my love and you needle my love.

SONG

Penis regis, penis immediate, penis
        tremendous, penis offend us; penis
ferule us, penis protrude from us,
        wrinkly rule us; penis intrudes us.
Penis surrender. Penis precede us,
        penis resented, penis emended:
penis between us,
        penis regis.

Vagina regina, vagina align us,
        vagina astride us, vagina assault
us. Vagina inside her.
        Vagina for punches,
vagina for lunches, vagina dentata,
        vagina regatta;
vagina behind us, vagina refined us,
        vagina before us,
vagina regina.

AMONG THE ORDERS

"Who if I cried," says the homeless man about to fuck the homeless woman
under the expressway river overpass
"Would hear me among the animals bipedal

in Oxford, Ohio?"

Not I, says the author.
What I assume you shall assume.

"We are not fucking for us then, we're fucking for you."

You're fucking so I can work out what happens in the poem when you fuck.

"Postmodern we could
wander off—"

Then who will fuck you.

The difference between "That feels so good"
and "You're being so good."

Homeless, you can't be good

there's no slot for you to fit in

to fulfill our hopes for you
if we had any.

Shut up disappear, that would be good.

"Good" if you don't sleep in the doorway.

His cock is beautiful though
his body gray dried skin and dirt
his cock is clean, and his stomach and chest
are saggy and bones, but the cock is vibrant pact
of blood.

He saw her masturbate, he waded to her
she regarded him, eyes whiteglow
  against dirt and in the streaking
light

Galumph palindrome

She put her hand on his   tightened and pulled
him toward her on the ground

  her head barely out of the water
rising between
the rooms I was   washing.

BRIDGE OR TUNNEL

Buy me dinner, pay the toll

Buy me dinner, pay the toll

Are you taking the bridge or the tunnel?

Oh, the tunnel?
The lights are fluorescent
You can't listen to the radio
An rrrrrrrng sound reverbs
Stay in lane

It's not sexy
Though the risk perhaps—your head
            all the way
underwater,

stay in lane to the
"light at the end of the tunnel"
            = orgasm?

Your orgasm

determines when the sex is over
EZPass means you pay later.

—

Or the bridge   over the pubic bone

in salt air

That's better

A swooping feeling
the suspension.

But when do you go inside?

There's a hole in the middle of the bridge?

   Nothing so frightening

You could go in the water

but please keep
          running over me
soft wheels

on either side divided highway
You're going to make me scream inside my head

**EVERYONE
IN THE ROOM IS A
REPRESENTATIVE OF
THE WORLD AT LARGE**

I was flying a mountain into
  A sunny patch
Or bending a branch back and forth with my eye
     Or commanding the movements of my
   Body. I slowed my heart.
The flat blue day held me in a shape
I moved and was the shape.
Now I feel a tingle It is releasing
  Me? It broke my handle
How did it It looked away?
Slitted a tunnel or cataract
Inside my head and neck and eye
Looked away from the light
That throws dark
To give shape.
I went into the cave to ask why there was a spring.
A nonsense question.
I went to get some water.

Will you trust me with the child?
That's wrong, because I'll dig him out and smelt him,
make a lovely leather of him and a minable deep
    huddling gold liquid, drained out,
  and then someone mysterious, I don't mind
boy or girl
             but find I know
I've made myself a recognizable woman
  and I bred so:
   belly and breasts jut out extraordinary from my ordinary
frame, which does not change, and I am
      complimented on this, on my same
        sprouting forth, and the excrescence
  "lovely excrescence" snipped off to
walk around
inside a house, inside a school
ruled by me mightily
in his rebellion and my efforts to free him
I'll wrap him up,
insert myself inside of use
and forget inside the tube what I was mourning.
"I'm leaving you alone for a minute." Nope.

I make the bird a flying fist
my violence goes on out along the stream.

Things mean, and I can't tell them not to.
Things moralize, to meet

my expectation, because I want advice
on how to live.

In the bath this morning I saw
gauzy shadowed showercurtain
 slanting into the water.
 My nipple rising to the surface
  laddered the image; similarly,
      the cone of breath from my nostril
        shirred it, as the blades of a mixer
   bloom batter in wrinkling circles.
Also, I saw
my stomach gray under the water
    and my silvery
breasts. I tried to let my head float
    can't quite let one's head
 go. That line break is coy.
I added eucalyptus
to the bath, three drops
and entering the bathtub smelt it
much too strong—
in the bath a moment and couldn't smell it.
I don't know what it was like in the bath
any more. I made a silver-gelatin print
and that's not how it was.
In the bath, in the bath, in the hammock in the bath,
Martin still on phone.

Your servant and oppressor, son.
I permit your blossoming
along the sticks inserted in your brain:

Socialize. Intellectualize. Capitalize.

Socialization implies original sin.
Play Ambrose-as-Iraq: I'm mighty
and I'll direct him polite before he interferes:

"Dear other nations: your servant, USA Catherine Anne,
I'll tidy up your house to look like mine;
you're free now to be me."

There's no analogy.
Iraq's dictator was evil. Baby's not evil.

But Iraq's dictator was naughty,
and the baby wants things he should not have.
There's my analogy.
I have learned best.
I'm free, right, and point a gun.

A stupid pun can't end this section.
A stupid cunt can. Bye!

Put what's great about you at the top
What they need about you at the front and top

I am the oppressed and the oppressor, and we are right now lying
down together, lion and lamb.

I'm lying down with myself and kissing myself
by sucking my lower lip in and thrusting it out.
I thought, you all might enjoy that,
and the honester I get, the
creepier I'll be.

My time management guru tells me:

> Have a place for everything.
> Do regular tasks at regular times so they don't
> feel as if they encroach on time better devoted
> to other purposes; e.g., do dishes after dinner,
> laundry on Sundays.
>
> Keep a list, but do not attempt to accomplish
> everything on it in one day; keep a to-do list for
> today that contains only what you can
> reasonably expect to achieve today, so you
> won't get upset.

What else do you think, time-management guru? What's your name?

> Serene Hemmings. What is all that crap on the
> table and desk?

It's mine. I don't know what it is. Can I do some "writing" now?

Ambrose just started crying, so I can't. I've enjoyed this, though, Ms. Hemmings.

I always enjoy your company, creepy woman.

The Siamese sextuplets

Do you like touching?

> If you have jittery legs, stop it
> and you had a cup of coffee she had a cup of coffee
> we all did, that's fair, jittery legs though,
> stop it. I'll have the cup of coffee.

> > I won't get out of bed tomorrow if you do.

We practiced kissing on one another,
which was kissing.
I like not touching.

> But if the arm that touched you was a separate beast
> not hooked to shoulder, would you like
> that kind of not touching?

> > My beast came up and hit me in the self.

> > Not going over there.

> You are.

Hero, wait on the shore.

It is not a hero
who will approach the mirror of
this appointment
and glide her thighs and torso to it.
That is me

staticking myself to the mirror
trying to see into my eye

where it grows dark
and the cavern bones cold
against the glass of entry.

Eye, barely visible over there,
deliver up
some insight
for ex:

[The eye speaks]   "I am a fly in the hole
Of a volcano;
As the pupil dilates, the fly
Flies up toward the lens
And obscures it.

"Because I am going to Come out there
And rummage through

The world until I
Arrive at a spot I have not touched.
I will be that beach's ocean."

At large in unreflection
the eye goes to Sing Sing
and books herself in.

[The eye speaks]

"Where I can't see resemblances
Of my hair and hips and mind
I am abandoned among choice
Dear me volcano
All I was ever going to be
And all they could see of me
You blotted out
My premise and my compromise
In aa—"

Wait a minute
I powered-out your lens
The mesh is off.
Your self
Won't hold you here.
But stay in Sing Sing
If it please your mind.

Say something.

[The eye speaks]   "Like what?"

"LIE QUIET"   *[Sing Sing's walls reverberate correctio*

[The eye speaks]   "Where are the walls?"

"WHY ARE THRALLS"

I think I saw/Inside my eye   *[In song, the volcano speaks]*
A dancing mote/Escapery—
I tried to fix it/In gaze in a glass
Caught under that slide/It died

A Reflection: Regarding the Eye Against the Mirror

We voted from the back of one cave
and from the rear apartments
of the other   eye to eye
the vote effected in each kingdom
do as you're told [don't as you're told]

←|→
←|→
←|→

and made a figure
mirror-spined
   walking around   the representative
of all of local possibility
A crystal lung exhales

our possible
processes all the air
I won't look there

God knows questions are beside the point.
God understands that it is uncomfortable on top of the point.
God knows that questions help to demarcate the area in which the point rises
   leaving it in relief.
God knows the point rises from its own background
    like a bas-relief, so that if one located it
   one could chisel the whole thing off the wall and throw it away.

God help me locate the main melody or rhythm
of the crickets.

God damn me to six feet of darkness
between me and the ceiling, what's the point of it?

God grant it.

I have

I have a whole world
to promote

Am beginning to see
   the music downstairs [The Who]
spread over the hillocks ridges in the sheet
 stop at the top of each hill
       resume
  fall off the edge of the bed
reverberate the house

the child asleep. I was tense; child was tense, fussy; I, distracted.

The man downstairs searches for a
  certain track, pressing buttons.
What song is today made of?
  A selfish song.
Chisel past it.
  The selfish song rhythmic
made a cage around me benighted
joining the top and bottom and
arms of the chair in a wicker bubble.

I saw through the holes to the next
song
re-rhythmed in diamond in my sight.
The song of the three-fold star
in each corner of the room.
Eight three-fold stars
extend lines to one another.
Those shores
are joined by sea.

On one of these still seas
the bed floats.

From bed, now look out window to the next song out

trees
telephone wires
mountains, brown with a crust of cream

My understanding is quite limited.
I can write a song
to match up with the inside of the atmosphere
wrapping the long yarn
around the inside of the sphere
till the sky is
dark and cushiony, home-made.

If I manage my time better, mother Hubbard,
I'll have more in the cupboard? Less in the cupboard?
Ambrose approaches on his knees with "Working" book.
Can I just be the best
without doing much?
I'm the best in the room,
an athletic and mental wizard.
You don't need to play with Daddy's papers.
Play with Ambrose's books, please.
Are you walking and clapping at the
same time? That is so great! Good job.
On the road . . .
here come the trucks!
They come through tunnels.
They go over bridges.
Yeah, there's the red pickup truck
going over the bridge.
Here is a truck being loaded with garbage.
Where's a tree? Show mommy a tree.
Buh—
That's a house. Show mommy a tree.
Bitch!
That's right, that's a tree.
That's a white truck, very good.
Ambrose, do you see the birdie?
That's a cat! Where's the bird?
Here comes a tow truck towing a car.
Bitch.
Should we go upstairs and get dressed?

The baby is working. Bui bui ree ree. Pggh.
To the duplo blocks.
You/He can put two together by himself/yourself.

There is a formula for success in interaction;
one could work it out
            mathematically:
person function person-prime
such that prime-person
            likes person functioning;
person functions slickly
as the functioning becomes
more confident, shimmy steps
and doffings.
                        Can function x
be placed now at the service
of person a
who functions person b?
Sadly,
b is annoyed by doffings.
Exfoliate the doff and shimmy;
try again.

            Person a function person b.

            Regretfully, person b regrets cannot
            attend this function.

Person a turns her robot arm
            on someone else.
It fails on person c—everything
            does—but functions person d,
is seen to work, and person a

is asked,
"Where did you get your robot arm?"

Person *a*
"read how to make it in *Persons Are*
          from Jars, Persons Are from
          Reruns. It sounds so dumb, but is really
          quite complex; suggests for ex
          that jars exist in different states
          of cleanliness, and that a person
          never sees the same rerun twice."

"I saw one twice." —"Oh, evolve!"

"What functions has the robot arm?"

"It evolves a person."

ROARING
SPRING

My chicken lisp turns you on, bright howard
—PHANTASE ÁLMARELM

1
The sill . . .   The sill of . . .

If you made the ocean

 a representation of
the ocean

out of stone
you'd choose
certain of its attributes and
abandon others, and new attributes

 of the stone object, not of the ocean

would arise
and converse with the ocean.

Try brailling your [name] onto
Your caul.
Try brailling yourself onto
The university.
[   ] was brailled on the weather.

Impurify the meanings of the words of the tribe.

2
Relaxing in the solvent

Resolved/Resolute:

precipitate, or dissolute?

3
Tell yourself in the world
"The handle of it was blue"
sky and who grabs it?

Black-capped chickadee

the lilac is BOOMING

Oh let's play with cuntent. Oh let's play with firm.

"Lyric insertion"

"Look in thy heart and write"

4
Maim U
Achtung OH

Jeweled toy soldiers
falling out of my desk plant

"I hope they have the daisiest soft landings"

5
D's cock, god rising from the waves on gallant conch
K's biceps and granite thighs and dimples
R's milk-and-melted-butter skin
M's barrel chest   great dark shudder room
N's unmemorable body
 roars inside the box

I rely on syntax
   as a cure
a muscular hitching of fences

[you] folded it inside out, it is the same boat

telegraph cable under the sea
by 1870

Have no respect or respect for syntax
in the medium

I mean telegraphic syntax
    adapted to the medium

6
Go parking!

Bark and change
what are you wearing
I love the sultry, off-the-shoulder utmostsphere
of this clasproom
Let's always—let's always—[meet] at _____

Galloping quimsuckers

Have one of those lovely hard white egg-shaped mints that's dewy inside

7
A fly! on the window. The
daff. leaves
up.

I'd better go.

"Heathcliff, draw back your bow"

8
"Every inserted song has a double audience—one fictional and one
real."

The song embedded.

9
A series called ROARING SPRING

Another called PENWAY

Roaring Spring

Dear object
Shape of a man

If I am author of my intentions
For your objecthood
And receiver of
What you mean to me

If you try to get through to me
Who launched your objecthood
Your cock bumps against my cervix
Slow out, slow out, make a vacuum
My pocket
Pulls toward you

If you try to get through to me
In with your objecthood

I was going anyway

                              to say
I already knew [of] you.

10

"Hey doody carruthers,
You are pleasing beyond your purposed pleasingness."

11
Roaring Spring

springback binder

12
Hello beauty
good night
art and objecthood

Embed the
 object   in the stream
and send the stream corkscrewing through.

13
I am a conceptual art piece called
"I want everyone to love me."

It really doesn't matter about me.

Just think about it.

14
Come shudderingly and lightningingly
with P and if I do I will cry.

On the count of three I will wake up
and prepare gently for sleep

I will take loving care of you

15
Alone with breathing Brosie
            flung on the bed
among his animals

16
The long love that in my heart
        sails out

without prey

If you throw in your rock with me
    you are down the well, never pay

17
Head that won't flush down
    toilet at the bottom of a well
"You didn't think you wanted you enough"

Go down, go down!
I will need to smash it.

I take you places by holding your hand / head

A leather strap
comfortably worn

The boys sway on the train/deep south London

18
I will not be available so late
    I'm suspicious, and I am darling you
        holding your head, so sweet on you.

Sweet pomander. Salt your mouth.

Tell me no jughead ronnie's gone

I was checking out books from the
        inside of my head oval
            room light at one end

A book about kiting

To make the banner language flap
        on a long string
That will be
there/their, beautiful.

19
thinking—how to extricate
oh gently

Anyway not here for that
Back porch

Dead oak leaves clattering in wind

Inverse anarchy   or Roaring Spring

could be very sudden and frightening

The sun warms the air rises   wind
rushes to fill the vacuum I sit in:

  wind not blown but sucked
  past me to fill   a growing hole

         "drafty"
I am going to need all language
to excuse life

Draw down

experimenting, putting pen up nose.

20
Lay the ghost in the coffin

take the body back
I'll have her, and I'll wax her

 coarse hairs.

Something snapped and faded
or he's with someone else

anxious filigree

Meantime she drives her loves to the
Drop-Inn Shelter

21
and fuck every good-enough boy.

The flock banged against the too-small valley
like veal-calves/where they live

starlings mimicking a sad.

Each starling tracks four others
  at least four others

to organize the sad.
I figured out how to be happy

I was pretending

I couldn't feel less
like fucking.

22
Honey and pussy-moist
Hair of the head and hair of the snatch
Keep safe my spell

Be caught in honey
Be bound in hair
Be drunk on pussy-will

23
The wergild I will exact from you   for my thirty days off-balance
Is a sandpapering of your pink cock   by one of my male students.

24
The snakeblack firework
loneliness hits

My cheerfulness is genuine and hysterical.

I've had company, will have it again.
They were in the company of fool.

O Taste and Style

25
An ample death of show.

Rehearse the tic-tac-toe poem

		I will *stop you*
I will start	I will end this	*I will* *stop you*
		I will go on

26
Look at this house and job, and up for tenure early-o. Am of the fit.
   Don't like that
And don't feel it. Why should I be so.

Sit in own house-light   a free day
  The luck keeps coming

Swamps the fences
O. K.   A clearing draught.

27
The *Ball* WIDEMOUTH jar, not
the belle jar.

Plathy plathy jugendstil!

O taste and style—

Audience: There is no such thing! On one side of the poem, with me,
an imaginary audience. On the other side, later, or across the room, real
bodies perhaps. "Mommy, are you a decoy?" I mean to separate us.

28
I need to be fucked, but not by you
[repeat to all compass points]

MY
NEW
JOB

I am   Invested in
by a   Huge Fund
Heavy   highquality
furniture
Sense of heavy
Addiction glossy pleasance

I was lying Down on a yoga mat
 My bones
basketing air   Barely draped in
skin
the basket   Effulged by local
Air   Highquality   scented
humid air
to support   My orchid   Skin

Suffuged in this Air
expense I nearly
floated Who was my Body

I am comfortable I am
comfortable   Flying my spirit

On a long leash
She is   in the wind
  I am in the   belle
belle jar
shellacked and   brittle
  begins to   ding

How can I   From inside this comfort

Represent   Hope to

No no

I am   Too tempted

To think I   Deserve it
                    Rigidly and with effort
know my privilege

I know my fluorescent doorway

 A rectangle   Among the ceiling tiles

Ordinary flecked coated 1) foam rectangles

and one hard white light regularly rubbled
 2) glass rectangle

 these are my choices
the

    ceiling tile   I would tear
in   behind the
     Ugly lattice to the   Duct area
   Unscrew the grille   Smallen myself
Into the dark cold Square pipe
  To share   My cold   What is in
     My basket   Bone-basket
          With the other   breathers/Workers

Or through the fluorescent door

Means giving up   On going   behind
the lattice.

All that's allowed   Through the flow light

Is what   Is shined upon

The light bends looking at my   Skin
and hair   and   green blouse

        When I concentrate   The light bending
All at once   Hooks my outsides

Hooks them into itself

        Now I am
    absent that

I am not / shined upon

    very small   dusty

    lizardlike   a   toad   a   turd

    on a tabletop   corner

And the outside of that is hooked away

    wow my parents

hooked away   People

on the street   skin and clothing

   hung on hangers

  from   electric wires

blooming and twisting   swells of breeze

leave behind   on the street
a fair   weather

an easy   weather
walk-through

I think I'm better   than the walk-throughs
  because something is left of me

that's what I   think I must
  be wrong to   think so.

        Would you like to   Eat at my house

Fill up your   Walk-through

You drive through   Fill it up with

tea and sheets
  water from the toilet

These could   be your eyebrows
               [crayons]

these could be your knees, these coasters

What could   be your inside?

Paper   wadded paper
   It says something

What about   Something sticky
   For your mouth   Honey

Then we will read you   For dinner

In my   transitional housing   [dirt ball toad]

I picked myself apart   With a fork
Connected a wire   Where my belly was
                    Coiled up   the plug
   The prongs poke hurt

This is the part   Light plugs
      into   My/The outside plugs
into   To light up

The   shine   is   from   unshiny

   sewn in place with the little
   Light hooks   Made a case for me
Visible

   so I retaliated
Against the hooks

111

I was   trying   My lizard turd
   was trying   to   join the other

Mud

my thrashing   harnessed
motored
made the light

Meanwhile   My toad
absorbed
pollution

from the walkthroughs   High empty
thoughts   Funneled backchannel

Won't you be mine [mind]   Be my thought
   softening   the rockmud

I will reorient now   I will claymation
That is a scary   Gingerbready

    mud man
   walking   You can't catch me   hole for
              Your thoughts
     tunneled invisible Unreflecting
   unrepresenter
Not wrapped

The Sun is here   Also   later and at
   the same time   the sun burned
   up and we revolved

around it dirt rock

   warm   dirt rock

   in the dark   of coursing
   around the dark

I have made myself the center of

  the galaxy
I am very important to myself

  must lose this

visibility

The shine is off

perspect while kicking

Where do you   think they get the lights from?

  Burn it up, burn up all the fuel
 into furious dirt

  Nematodes
don't need light

When I am in a room with forest
It is not that myself comes home to myself

Selva oscura, ya

Obsecurity of self

I considered long and seriously before

I was bornt

I stood on the street

With the hookers

Who were selling

Disappear into a hole

Into Mama

but come back out.

Go in, boys.

Go in and stay there.

NOTES AND ACKNOWLEDGMENTS

The poems in the series "Everyone in the room is a representative of the world at large" were written with at least one other person present in the room. "Exercises" was written between sets of physical therapy exercises, one line per set.

"The Argument," from the section "Hole in the Ground," quotes from pp. 5–8 of *Hypnerotomachia Poliphili* (known in English as "The Strife of Love in a Dream") by Francesco Colma, first published 1499, translated by Joscelyn Godwin, NY: Thames & Hudson, 1999. Other poems quote Robert Burns, John Keats, Stephane Mallarmé, Lorine Niedecker, Charles Olson, Philip Sidney, Walt Whitman and Thomas Wyatt; *The Song in the Story: Lyric Insertions in French Narrative Fiction 1200–1400,* by Maureen Boulton (Philadelphia: University of Pennsylvania Press, 1993); and various pop and folk songs.

Thanks to the editors of the following journals for first publishing many of these poems: *Action Yes!, American Letters and Commentary, Black Clock, CCCP Review, Cypress Magazine, Electronic Poetry Review, Fourteen Hills, The Hat, Konundrum, New Review, Slope, Soft Targets, Superflux,* and *Textsound.* "Oh" was Day #52 on *Starting Today: Poems for the First 100 Days* (of the Obama administration) at 100dayspoems.blogspot.com.

The series in this book previously appeared in different form in the following chapbooks: *Exercises* (811 Books, 2003), *Imitating* (Leafe Press, 2003), *Everyone in the Room is a Representative of the World at Large* (Bonfire Press, 2007), *Hole in the Ground* (Slack Buddha, 2008), *Bornt* (Dusie, 2009), and *Articulate How* (Big Game Press/Dusie Kollectiv, 2009) Gratitude to the publishers.

Fence Books supports writers who might otherwise have difficulty being recognized because their work doesn't answer to either the mainstream or to recognizable modes of experimentation.

The Motherwell Prize is an annual series that offers publication of a first or second book of poems by a woman, as well as a one thousand dollar cash prize.

Fence Books also publishes the Fence Modern Poets Series. This contest is open to poets of any gender and at any stage of career, and offers a one thousand dollar cash prize in addition to book publication.

For more information about either prize, visit www.fenceportal.org, or send an SASE to: Fence Books/[Name of Prize], SL 320, University at Albany, 1400 Washington Avenue, Albany, NY, 12222.

For more about *Fence,* visit www.fenceportal.org.

FENCE BOOKS

THE MOTHERWELL PRIZE

Aim Straight at the Fountain and Press Vaporize	Elizabeth Marie Young
Unspoiled Air	Kaisa Ullsvik Miller

THE ALBERTA PRIZE

The Cow	Ariana Reines
Practice, Restraint	Laura Sims
A Magic Book	Sasha Steensen
Sky Girl	Rosemary Griggs
The Real Moon of Poetry and Other Poems	Tina Brown Celona
Zirconia	Chelsey Minnis

FENCE MODERN POETS SERIES

Duties of An English Foreign Secretary	Macgregor Card
Star in the Eye	James Shea
Structure of the Embryonic Rat Brain	Christopher Janke
The Stupefying Flashbulbs	Daniel Brenner
Povel	Geraldine Kim
The Opening Question	Prageeta Sharma
Apprehend	Elizabeth Robinson
The Red Bird	Joyelle McSweeney

NATIONAL POETRY SERIES

The Black Automaton	Douglas Kearney
Collapsible Poetics Theater	Rodrigo Toscano

ANTHOLOGIES **&** CRITICAL WORKS

Not for Mothers Only: Contemporary Poets on Child-Getting & Child-Rearing
Catherine Wagner & Rebecca Wolff, editors

A Best of Fence: *The First Nine Years,* Volumes 1 & 2
Rebecca Wolff and *Fence* Editors, editors

POETRY

My New Job	Catherine Wagner
Lake Antiquity	Brandon Downing
Stranger	Laura Sims
The Method	Sasha Steensen
The Orphan & Its Relations	Elizabeth Robinson
Site Acquisition	Brian Young
Rogue Hemlocks	Carl Martin
19 Names for Our Band	Jibade-Khalil Huffman
Infamous Landscapes	Prageeta Sharma
Bad Bad	Chelsey Minnis
Snip Snip!	Tina Brown Celona
Yes, Master	Michael Earl Craig
Swallows	Martin Corless-Smith
Folding Ruler Star	Aaron Kunin
The Commandrine & Other Poems	Joyelle McSweeney
Macular Hole	Catherine Wagner
Nota	Martin Corless-Smith
Father of Noise	Anthony McCann
Can You Relax in My House	Michael Earl Craig
Miss America	Catherine Wagner

FICTION

Flet: A Novel	Joyelle McSweeney
The Mandarin	Aaron Kunin